The Mystery of the ANCIENT ANCHOR

The Mystery *of the* ANCIENT ANCHOR

by Matt Price

BEACON HILL PRESS
OF KANSAS CITY

Copyright 2010
by Beacon Hill Press of Kansas City

Printed in the United States of America

ISBN 978-0-8341-2490-5

Cover Design: Darlene Filley
Illustrator: Dorris Ettinger
Interior Design: Sharon Page

Editor: Donna Manning
Assistant Editor: Laura Lohberger

Note: This sequel to *The Secret of High Horse Castle* is based on the experiences of the author, missionary Matt Price, while in language training in France.

10 9 8 7 6 5 4 3 2 1

Contents

1. Rolling for a Win!   7

2. Loading Up the Car   12

3. Ready to Hit the Road   15

4. On the Right Track   17

5. A Break for Bratwurst   21

6. A Stop in Strasbourg   24

7. River Ride Interrupted   30

8. The Ancient Anchor   34

9. Searching for Clues   40

10. Roaming the Ruins   44

11. The Final Clue   50

12. Almost Home   55

1
Rolling for a Win!

"Keep rolling, keep rolling, YES!" shrieked Franko, watching his ball roll to within an inch of the marker.

"How do you do that?" asked Lucas.

Lucas rolled three balls, but none of them landed anywhere close to the marker. Franko rolled each of his three as if they were drawn to a magnet. The boys were playing a popular European game known as petanque [peh-TAHNK] or boules [BOOLZ].

The game is played with balls about the size of a billiard ball. The goal of this game is simple. Two to four players roll three balls toward a small marker ball. The player rolling a ball closest to the marker ball wins the round. It is common to see a serious player checking the distance between his or her ball and the marker with a tape measure.

Franko collected the three green balls and the small white ball used as a marker. Lucas sauntered after the purple-colored balls. Since Franko won the last round, it was his chance to throw the marker ball.

"Here it goes," yelled Franko, throwing the marker ball over his head and behind him. It landed 15 feet from where they were standing in the city park. Every

small town in France has a flat area used for playing petanque. It is usually found in a central location downtown.

Lucas was the first to toss the ball. He stood at the imaginary line from where Franko threw the marker. He eyed the marker and threw the ball underhanded like a softball. The ball curved upward in a gentle arch before dropping toward the marker. It hit the ground, bounced, and rolled past the marker by 10 inches. Lucas smiled at Franko as if to say, "Try to beat that one."

Franko winked back, "Good one, my friend." Without breaking stride, Franko swung back his arm and let loose the ball. It sailed through the air and landed directly on top of Lucas's ball, knocking it away from the marker.

"Hey! You can't do that," complained Lucas.

"Yes, you can," replied Franko. "It's in the rules. One ball can hit the other as long as it does not hit the marker ball."

Lucas grumbled, "That's just one way to view the rules. I wish these rules were a lot more firm."

Lucas went on to roll two more times without getting even close to the marker. With a small amount of effort, Franko easily won the round. As they were lining up for another round, a boy with dark brown hair and brown eyes walked up to Lucas and Franko.

"Hello," said the boy. "My name is Miguel. Miguel Hector Estrada. We just moved here from Guatemala [gwah-tuh-MAH-luh] so my parents can study French. We live down the street at the language school."

"I live at the same school with my parents," said Lucas. "Why did you come in the middle of November instead of the beginning of the school year?"

"Visa problems," recited Miguel as if he had told this story often. "It took a long time for my parents to receive the right visa from the French government. But now we're here. Visitors traveling to most countries in Europe must have visas. That controls how many people can enter the country. I know because my father worked for the Guatemalan government before he became a Christian. He helped process visa applications for people visiting Guatemala."

"How did you learn to speak French so well?" asked Lucas, struggling with his own French accent.

"My father worked for one year in a company in Belgium. Many of my friends spoke both French and English. So I learned a lot while we were there." Miguel turned to Lucas and asked, "By the way, are you an American?"

"Yes, I'm an American," replied Lucas with a grin. "But how did you know?"

"Because of your accent," said Miguel.

Lucas shook his head, smiling. Franko nodded in agreement, and then turned his attention back to the task at hand.

"I'm glad you are visiting my country," said Franko, his eyes brightening. "Do you want to join us for a game of petanque?"

"Sure," said Miguel. "How do you play?"

Franko and Lucas explained the rules. They had an extra set of red-colored balls for Miguel to use. The boys let Miguel take the first turn. They realized quickly that he knew how to play and play well.

Miguel's first two throws were only a few inches from the marker, and one of them was closer to the marker than Franko's. As Lucas glanced toward Miguel, he had to admit that Franko might have met his match at petanque.

"Where did you learn how to play like this?" Franko asked Miguel.

Lucas thought Franko sounded worried. He wondered if Miguel might unseat Franko as the reigning champ in today's game.

Miguel replied to Franko, "I learned how to play horseshoes with my American friends in Belgium. This game is not much different."

Franko knew nothing about the game of horseshoes. And he hoped Miguel would not be able to remember any tips from the game to help him in petanque. Before that could happen, Franko turned everyone's attention back to the game.

"OK, let's roll the last ball," Franko said, making way for Miguel. "Be my guest."

2
Loading Up the Car

"I'm here, Lucas!" yelled Amina [ah-MEE-nah], as she ran from her father's car.

"OK, but don't forget your bags," called Lucas. "They're still in the backseat."

Amina's father had a broad smile under his bushy mustache. "Here they are, my dear," said Mr. Azaz [AH-zahz]. Then he pulled not one, but two overstuffed suitcases from the backseat of his car.

"I've got to hurry, Amina," her father said hastily. "My train to Geneva leaves right away. Have fun with your friends, and I'll see you in a few days." He gave Amina a quick hug, jumped back into his car, and drove away. Meanwhile, Lucas was staring at Amina's luggage in disbelief.

"Amina, where do you think you're going?" he asked jokingly.

"What do you mean?" asked Amina. "I'm going on vacation break with your family."

"I know, but we'll only be there for five days," replied Lucas, grinning. "That's enough baggage for two weeks."

"Hmm! Maybe for a boy," Amina snapped, flipping her hair.

Just then, the Estradas arrived, and Miguel scrambled out of the car.

Amina grabbed her suitcases and strutted past Lucas toward his father's car.

"What did I say?" asked Lucas.

"What *did* you say?" Miguel asked, as he joined Lucas. "She looks really irritated. Maybe you should be taking Franko with us on the trip instead."

"I wish all of us could go," said Lucas sadly. "It will be the first vacation break I've spent without Franko."

"Why couldn't he go with us?" asked Miguel.

"The trip cost too much money," said Lucas. "We have to take the train, and it's too expensive for Franko. Besides, I think he has to help his mother at the Christmas market. I figure Mama Falco couldn't be without her extra set of hands for a week."

"I'm sorry he can't go," said Miguel. "But my family is looking forward to seeing more of Europe. I can't wait to visit Mulhouse [muh-LOOZ], Strasbourg [STRAHS-boorg], Basel [BAH-zuhl], and Geneva [juh-NEE-vuh]. By the way, did you know that French and Swiss people on the German border speak more German than anything else? Do you know German?"

"Nein [NAH-een]," replied Lucas. "It means 'no' in German."

Out of the corner of his eye, Lucas saw Amina toss one suitcase, and then a second one, into the arms of a surprised Mr. Caster.

"It looks like Amina is still a little upset," said Miguel.

"I'm still not sure what I said," replied Lucas. "But I'm sure she'll get over it. I better go help my dad finish loading the car."

Miguel cautiously approached Amina. "Good morning."

"Is it?" quizzed Amina. She rolled her dark eyes and gave her long black hair a toss.

"Well, maybe not. Just thought I'd say hello," answered Miguel, trying to think quickly of something else to talk about. "Are you looking forward to the trip? Have you been to Switzerland and Germany before?"

"Loads of times," said Amina. "My father goes to Geneva all the time because of his work as a doctor."

"Oh, I didn't know your dad was a doctor," Miguel said. "What kind of doctor is he?"

"He tries to find ways to fight sickness in places like Africa and Asia," explained Amina. "I think I want to be a doctor like him. Sometimes I go with him."

Miguel asked, "Do you miss him when you can't go with him?"

Amina nodded, holding back tears.

"It will be OK," said Miguel. "Lucas's parents are great people, and my family will love getting to know you. Besides, it will only be a few days before we drop you off in Geneva on our way back from Germany."

Amina smiled, "Thanks, Miguel. I needed to hear that. I better go say sorry to Lucas for being so grumpy."

"I'll go with you," said Miguel, turning to follow her. "Hey, where did all the luggage go?"

3
Ready to Hit the Road

"Are you two all set and ready to go?" Lucas grinned as he watched Amina and Miguel approach the fully loaded Caster family car.

"You're done loading the car already?" asked Miguel. "I was going to help you."

Looking in the rear window of the hatchback, Amina said, "I can't believe you fit all of the luggage into that small spot. That's enough luggage for five people—and it's for only four of us."

"Well, if you'd packed and moved as much as I have, you'd be able to pack the same way," Lucas admitted. "It's not a gift or anything, just a way of life for us. My dad was a pastor before we moved here as missionaries."

"What do pastors do?" asked Amina.

"Oh, they take care of people. They preach and teach. They pray for people when they are hurting. And they help them when they are in trouble."

Amina stared blankly at Lucas.

"Oh, yeah, I forgot you were born in a country without a lot of churches," continued Lucas. "Pastors help people understand the Bible better when they preach. They help people understand God better when they pray."

Miguel piped in, "Pastors like my father make it easier for people in church to help people outside the church. He has to be there when a family is in trouble, even in the middle of the night. Pastors usually spend a lot of time away from home. I wish my father was with us more often, but I feel good that he is helping others."

"I didn't realize there were people doing things like that," Amina responded.

"There are lots of pastors around the world," said Lucas. "My father and Miguel's are going to Africa to help train pastors there."

Amina replied, "It's kind of like what my father does as a doctor—only he helps people's bodies get better."

Lucas added, "Our fathers help people get better spiritually."

"What does 'spiritually' mean?" asked Amina.

"That might take a while to explain," said Miguel, smiling.

"You're right," said Lucas. "We can talk more about it once we catch the train. We must be about ready to leave. Once my dad is ready, he wants to go right away."

Miguel responded, "My father had us pack the car early this morning. We tend to be more relaxed about time."

"I wish the trains were that way," said Amina. "They don't wait for anyone, no matter where they are from or where they are going."

4
On the Right Track

"Hurry up, Lucas!" shouted Amina. "Miguel and his family are already on the train. Your family is lagging behind."

Lucas wiped the sweat from his forehead even though the air was cool.

"We're coming! Hold table seats for us!" cried out Lucas, running toward the entrance to the train station. "We're carrying luggage for five people, remember?"

"OK, I'll grab a suitcase. Let's just hurry," said Amina.

"We'll make the train," assured Mr. Caster. "We always make it, maybe not early, but we always make it."

Lucas trailed behind all of them with suitcases in both hands and a bag hanging on each shoulder.

"You're lucky you didn't trip," giggled Amina, as they settled into their seats facing each other on the train.

"What do you mean?" asked Lucas, half-knowingly. "Just because my shoes were untied?"

"You should learn to tie your shoes correctly," Amina teased.

"And, how is that?" quizzed Lucas. "It's not like I haven't been tying my shoes since I was five years old."

"Well, you should tie them like you don't want them to dangle under your feet all the time," responded Amina.

"What are you two arguing about now?" asked Miguel, winking at Lucas. "Almost as bad as my aunt and uncle back home—always arguing about nothing."

Lucas blushed three shades of red and tried to slide deeper into his seat.

"We made it on time, didn't we?" said Miguel, reciting the time of departure. He plopped into the facing seat on the other side of the fold-down table. "Seventeen-twenty-three." France and other countries in Europe give travel times using the 24-hour clock: 17:23 means 5:23 in the afternoon.

Amina returned to the previous subject, "I was just letting Lucas know that he needed to tie his shoes better. He could have tripped and broken his nose back at the train station."

"Haven't I tried to tell you the same thing, Lucas?" started Miguel.

Before Miguel could launch into a minilecture, Lucas suggested, "Let's play a game or something. How about the game called Snitch? I brought it with me. What do you think?"

"I think it's a great idea," agreed Amina. "As long as you double tie your shoelaces. And then both of you can tell me more about what the word 'spiritual' means."

"We'd be glad to do that," said Miguel with a smile. "Being spiritual means being friends with God and making that the most important part of your life. It means learning to love God, and also love the things that God loves. People who are spiritual don't think *only* about having things like food, clothes, fame, or lots of money. They want to be part of God's bigger world, and so they focus on that.

"What do you mean 'God's bigger world'?" asked Amina, looking confused.

"It's . . . well, it's . . . it's hard to explain," said Lucas thoughtfully. "But we're talking about loving God and being part of His family."

"It's all in the Bible," added Miguel eagerly. "The Bible tells us how God made the world, and people, and everything. He is the ruler of the whole world—even though most people don't know it. And everyone in the whole world who learns to know and love God becomes part of His family—which will last forever and ever. And we will live forever too."

"I'm not sure I understand," replied Amina. "I've never heard of anything like this before."

"Think of it this way," said Lucas. "Think about how the three of us are friends. We talk together, and try to learn new things about each other, and we do nice things for each other." Then he laughed. "Well *sometimes* we do nice things for each other. Anyway, that's sort of what spiritual people do with God."

"In his sermons, my dad talks about *walking with God*," added Miguel. "It's not that you actually take walks with Him . . . but you think about Him, and love Him, and learn to do what pleases Him."

"And that takes discipline," said Lucas. "That's what my father says in *his* sermons. It's kind of like our trains—they stay on the tracks instead of going just anywhere. But we don't have to do this all by ourselves.

God gives us all kinds of help—like the Bible, church, Christian friends . . . and His Spirit living in us."

"I think I'm beginning to get it . . . sort of," said Amina. "Can you tell me more about this later on? Right now, I want to play Snitch."

"Sure," said Lucas and Miguel at the same time.

5

A Break for Bratwurst

"Lucas, are you awake?" asked Miguel.

Lucas opened his eyes. All he saw was a blur of passing scenery outside the foggy train windows. He started to close his eyes again, when . . .

"Lucas!" said Miguel, more sharply this time. "You've got to wake up. We're almost to Mulhouse. I'm tired too. We stayed up way too long last night playing Snitch and talking to Amina. But I think she's beginning to understand what we were talking about."

"I hope so," sighed Lucas, trying to get his eyes to stay open for more than a few seconds. "I have a feeling there will be more questions."

Miguel yawned. "It's been a long ride."

"Boys, let's get ready for our transfer in Mulhouse," Mr. Caster reminded them as he walked down the aisle. "We will have a couple of hours before we catch our next train, so we thought we would go into town and see the outdoor market."

"Come on, Amina," said Lucas, tapping her on the shoulder. "It's time to get off this train. We're going to visit the market in Mulhouse while we wait on our next train."

21

Miguel joined them as they exited the train with their backpacks. They followed the Casters and Estradas out of the train station.

"Let's stick together," said Mr. Estrada. "I don't want to be looking for you when we should be getting back on our train."

"OK," said the three in unison. They walked together a few steps in front of their parents. They soon found themselves in the market.

"Feel this beautiful cloth," Amina said, touching the soft fabrics hanging at a storefront.

"Yeah, I guess it's soft," said Lucas, never having paid much attention before now to fabrics.

The group made their way through the narrow streets of downtown Mulhouse. They visited the many stalls covered with the dangling, colorful fabrics for which this town is known.

"I'm getting kind of hungry," said Lucas. The families agreed to stop at a small café.

"Look at all the sausages," said Miguel. "I don't think they have anything else."

"This is the Alsace [al-SAS] region," Amina explained. "It is known for sausages and sauerkraut. This town was once part of Germany."

"It's not as good as corn tortillas and chicken," said Miguel. "But I'm hungrier than a dog gone blind."

Lucas and Amina stared blankly at Miguel.

"That's just one way that we say 'I'm really hungry' in Guatemala," offered Miguel.

"Oh," said Amina, nodding along with Lucas.

"I'd say, 'I'm so hungry I could eat a horse,'" added Lucas, rubbing his stomach.

"I didn't know people thought horses tasted so good," said Amina, repulsed by the thought.

"I didn't say I *would* eat one, but that I *could* eat something as big as a horse," said Lucas. "Besides, it's just a saying."

"And I say, let's quit talking and eat," concluded Miguel. The kids quickly found seats near their parents' table.

"This food is so good," said Amina between bites. "I've never had sauerkraut on a sausage before. What did you call this piece of meat? A hot dog?"

"Yes. Although people in the United States would call a hot dog this big a bratwurst," Lucas replied. Then he added, "The sauerkraut is a little too sour for me, and the French bread makes it sort of chewy."

"Pass the hot mustard, please," said Miguel, starting on his second French-style hot dog.

"Are you trying to say you don't like it, Lucas?" prodded Amina.

"I'm just comparing this food to what I know," shrugged Lucas. Then he said with a smirk, "I've definitely got room for at least one more after I finish this one."

Before Lucas had time to order a second hot dog, Mr. Caster hurried to their table. "It's time to get back to the Mulhouse station. We don't want to miss the train."

Lucas, Amina, and Miguel hurried along with the parents to the train station. When they arrived, they found the train with a number matching the one on their tickets. They rushed into a car and found seats together. The soft tones of the train signal echoed in the station as they began moving. Before they could think of something else to talk about, they drifted into a nap one by one.

6

A Stop in Strasbourg

Lucas read the sign as they pulled into the next train station. "Strasbourg. Hey guys, we are here."

"Here? Already?" said Amina, sleepily.

Miguel yawned, trying to wake up. "Strasbourg? I thought we just left Mulhouse."

"Time flies when you're fast asleep," said Lucas, standing up slowly.

In the train station, Mr. Caster gathered them around. "We have a few hours before our next train departs," he said. "Let's see the famous pink cathedral and visit some shops."

Everyone nodded in agreement and headed for the station exit.

"The streets are a lot more crowded here," Miguel pointed out.

"This is a lot bigger city," said Amina as she looked around. "I saw a sign back there listing important offices in the European Parliament. I remember my father saying that he studied medicine here. It's where Louis Pasteur [LOO-ee pas-TUHR] is from."

"Who is he?" asked Lucas.

"You know about pasteurized milk, don't you?" asked Miguel, and Lucas nodded positively. "Louis Pasteur invented a way to prepare milk so it would not make people sick from germs."

"Yuck!" blurted Amina. "I don't want to think about what it was like before his invention."

"That's a very good point," agreed Miguel. "In those times, if two glasses of milk were served, they both might look the same. They could even taste the same. However, what was not known and could not be seen was the fact that one of the glasses of milk could be full of deadly germs."

"This reminds me of our conversation about spirituality," said Lucas. "Just like germs in milk are deadly, so is sin in our lives. Like the germs that grow unseen in milk, sin is unseen in our hearts. Sin is deadly because it separates us from God. When Jesus comes into our lives, though, He deals with our sins and makes it possible for us to have a relationship with God."

"Yeah. It's sort of like being 'pasteurized' by the Spirit," added Miguel, as Amina listened closely.

"Definitely," said Lucas. "Hey, look at the sign on this hotel. It says that Gutenberg [GOO-ten-buhrg] lived in Strasbourg for some time."

"Who is Gutenberg?" asked Amina.

"He invented the first printing press in the 1400s. Without him, there would be no books in print. One of the first books he printed was the Bible. I remember learning about it in history class last year," explained Miguel.

"I thought there were Bibles a long time before that," said Amina.

"There were, but they had to be written by hand," said Miguel. "They were rare and expensive. Gutenberg made it possible for many people to have Bibles. My dad said it was an invention that changed the world, because more people could read and share with each other. It's kind of like what the Internet does for us today."

Just then the group turned the corner from the cobblestone alley and entered the square.

Amina gasped, "Whoa! Look at that!"

In the middle of the square stood Strasbourg's giant cathedral.

"That is one a-mazing building," said Lucas. His eyes followed the cathedral to the top of the single 500-foot spire.

Miguel silently nodded in agreement.

"It's beautiful," said Amina softly. "Look at the rose-colored reflection off the stone walls."

"That's not a reflection," said Mrs. Caster. "That's the actual color. How did the stones get to be so . . . pink?"

"Let's go ask someone," suggested Mrs. Estrada. "There's a tourist over there with a guidebook."

"Good idea," chimed in Mrs. Caster.

After a brief discussion with the tourist, the ladies came back. "It's rose-colored sandstone," they reported.

Lucas looked at the cathedral and said, "I wonder how they brought all those huge stones from the mountains miles and miles away. That must have been exhausting work."

"I can't wait to go inside," exclaimed Amina, as they all headed toward the huge arched doorways.

"We have to pay to go in?" questioned Miguel, staring at a notice board near the door. "Can they be serious? Do we have to pay to enter a church?"

Lucas elbowed Miguel gently and said softly, "Just pay the money and don't cause a scene."

"I think it is wrong to pay to go into a church. It's God's house," challenged Miguel.

"We'll pay the fee," said the Casters and the Estradas, handing the entrance fees to the elderly matron at the door. "It's probably to keep this place looking clean."

"You don't have to pay for me," said Amina.

"We know we don't have to, but we want to," said Mrs. Caster, leading the group into the sanctuary with its towering columns.

"The windows are so colorful and beautiful," admired Amina. "And look at the statues. Who are they supposed to be?"

"I think they represent the really spiritual people who lived ages ago," said Miguel. "My dad was raised as a Catholic, so he knows more about the statues than I do."

"You explained things correctly, Son," said Mr. Estrada. "Also, the stained-glass windows tell stories about people in the Bible. It was a way for people who couldn't read to see the Bible stories with their own eyes."

Miguel pointed upward. "Look at how tall the organ pipes are. I bet they are really loud."

Lucas and Amina nodded. Then Lucas said, "It's a lot colder in here than outside. It's sort of strange. Listen to the echo of our footsteps on the stone. It's like walking through a cave."

"I think this building is grand," said Amina as she, Lucas, and Miguel wandered down a long aisle. "I would enjoy staying in here all day. But it is also very empty. Why aren't there more people here?"

"You're right," Miguel said. "There aren't many people here. But I hope it's full of people during a worship service."

"I don't think I've ever been in a place that seemed so sacred," said Amina reverently.

"Then what's wrong, Amina?" asked Miguel. "Are you crying? I see a tear."

"I don't know," said Amina, wiping the tears from her eyes. "It's just so beautiful in here. I have never been in a place like this before. It seems like all the answers you've been giving to my questions are starting to make sense."

Lucas exchanged a glance with Miguel, who smiled. "Well then, come on, Amina. If you want to know more about God, we can help. But if you want to know God, you can talk to Him directly."

"How?" asked Amina, her eyes still full of tears.

"Like this," said Miguel, grabbing Amina and Lucas's hands and standing in a circle. Then they prayed for Amina. It was the first time the three of them had prayed together, and the first time Amina had prayed.

Outside the cathedral, Amina wore a big smile across her face. Lucas waved to his parents across the square.

"What happened to you in there?" asked Mrs. Estrada, as everyone gathered around.

"I . . .I met God for the first time," said Amina shyly. "And it was wonderful."

Everyone gave Amina a big hug.

Miguel quietly thanked God for meeting with them in His cathedral.

7

River Ride Interrupted

"So, this is Basel," said Miguel, looking down at the street from his second-floor hotel window.

DING! DING! DING!

"Lucas, come and look at the tram (streetcar) going down the middle of the street," Miguel called.

Lucas ran to the window just in time to see people who were riding bicycles and pushing carts scrambling to each side of the road. The tram was filled to capacity with people. It was guided by the electrical wires above and the tracks below as it moved slowly down the street.

Suddenly, there was a pounding at their door.

"Hey, are you guys awake in there?" yelled Amina, as she rapped on the door to their room.

"We're awake," said Miguel, as he opened the door.

Amina smiled and greeted them. "Good morning. Your parents sent me to tell you that the rest of us are ready. We're downstairs eating breakfast on the first level."

"OK, we're coming," assured Lucas.

"Remember, we're going on a riverboat ride," said Amina. "We'll be leaving soon for the dock. See ya downstairs. Hurry!"

Ten minutes later, the boys arrived for breakfast. They were out of breath from running down three steep flights of stairs.

"Did you leave any toast and jam for us?" asked Miguel.

"Of course," said his father. "It's on the counter along with the juice."

Lucas and Miguel filled their plates and plopped them down at a wobbly table for two. Amina and the four adults were just finishing their breakfast.

Five minutes later the whole gang left the hotel. They walked toward the dock where they boarded the ferryboat.

Amina, Lucas, and Miguel stood along the rail watching as the boat was steered into the river. The green hull of the boat splashed into the river current.

Amina shivered in the cool breeze. She wished she had her sweater.

They had not been on the boat very long when Lucas and Miguel saw someone waving frantically on the riverbank. At that moment, the boat lurched to starboard (toward the left side). Miguel grabbed the rail to keep from falling into the water. And Amina screamed as the boat vibrated violently.

Lucas heard the captain yell orders to crew members on the deck. They ran to the bow (front) of the boat. One of them dropped the anchor. Soon the chain released the anchor and stretched tightly. The out-of-control boat was secured to the muddy river bottom. Sirens wailed from the streets along the river.

Smaller paddle boats soon arrived to shuttle the people to the shore. Ambulances and emergency workers helped injured passengers. No one suffered anything more serious than bruises and small cuts. The Casters, Estradas, and Amina waited patiently for their turn to get on a rescue boat. In 15 minutes they were safely on solid ground.

"I can't believe what just happened," exclaimed Amina to the two boys.

"I can't either," agreed Miguel.

Lucas added, "That was more adventure than I hoped for today."

"I almost took a dive into the river," admitted Miguel.

"And you didn't even bring a swimming suit," teased Lucas.

Miguel rolled his eyes but kept smiling.

"I'm just glad we're all OK," said Amina.

The two fathers walked over to the children. Miguel's father said, "The tour operator has canceled the rest of the boat rides for today."

"What are we going to do now?" asked Miguel.

Lucas joked, "I hope it's something on dry ground."

"I think we can all agree to that suggestion, Lucas," said his dad. "We parents think it would be a good idea to take the train to Kaiseraugst [kie-zuhr-AH-guhst]. It's just up the river from where we are here in Basel. There we can see the Roman ruins. Maybe we will have a little less excitement."

Miguel jumped to his feet, and helped Amina and Lucas to theirs.

"As long as we don't go roamin' too far away from our plan," joked Lucas.

8
The Ancient Anchor

"Well, at least the train was a lot less scary than the ferryboat," stated Miguel.

Amina and Lucas agreed as they walked down a narrow lane in Kaiseraugst.

The parents agreed to allow the three friends to explore the neighborhood while they scoured a used bookstore.

"Hey, guys, I'm thirsty," said Amina. "There's a place that might have a café mocha. My insides are still shaking from what happened on the boat."

Lucas wrinkled his nose. "I don't know how you can drink coffee. But I'm thirsty too. I could use a Coke."

"You're such an American!" taunted Amina playfully. "Always drinking Coke."

"But both of you could be lots healthier if you would drink plenty of agua [AH-gwah] (Spanish for water)," Miguel retorted. "Like us Guatemalans."

"Look. There's an inn with a café," said Lucas. "Maybe we can find something to drink there." He pointed across the lane to the small sign hanging between two flags with a glass lamp on one side. The sign above a blue door read, *Die Alten Anker* [die AHL-ten ANG-ker].

Amina said, "Let's go in and see what they have."

Lucas swung open the door for Miguel and Amina.

"Wow! There's a strong smell in here," said Miguel.

Amina inhaled deeply. "Mmm, fresh ground coffee!" she said.

"I love that smell too," admitted Lucas. "I just can't stand the taste. It's too bitter."

WWWRRRR! The woman behind the counter worked the grinding espresso machine. Two other people sat in the dimly lit room. The wooden floor creaked as the three friends passed by the polished counter. They chose a table with three chairs scattered about. The woman and the two other customers glanced in their direction as they sat down.

"Did you see how those two men looked at us when we came in?" asked Amina.

"Yes," said Lucas. "This place seems a little spooky."

The woman whisked from behind the counter, a long calico dress whipping about her black, high-heeled boots. She placed two steaming espressos on the small table where the two men sat, and then turned to the kids.

"Guten tag [GOO-ten TAHK] (Good day), Bonjour [bo-ZHUR] (Good day), Good day, my young friends. My name is Hilga. I'm the owner of this café and inn." The three friends listened in amazement as she introduced herself in German, French, and English. "What will you have today?" the inn owner inquired.

"I would like a café mocha, please," answered Amina.

"I'll take a Coke," Lucas replied.

Miguel answered, "I just want agua, I mean water."

"Very good. I will be right back."

Amina whispered, "Did you notice that she didn't even look at those two creepy-looking men over there?"

"I wonder who they are, and what they are doing," said Miguel.

"Probably up to no good," judged Lucas. "Hilga looks scared of them."

CLUNK! CLUNK! The two men dressed in long gray coats dropped their coins on the table and left the café.

Hilga carried a tray from behind the counter, glancing nervously at the door where the men exited.

"Here are your drinks. No charge for the water."

Amina pulled money from her jeans pocket to pay for the café mocha and Coke. "Here you go." She paused. "Umm, Madame Hilga, who were those men? You look scared. Did they threaten you?"

"No, dear," said Hilga. "I am not frightened, and they did not threaten me. At least, not directly."

"What does 'not directly' mean?" questioned Lucas. "Sorry, I don't mean to pry."

"I will answer you," continued Hilga. "The men came in here two days ago and told me I would have to close this inn. They want to tear it down to build a parking lot. I told them that the inn is a historical site. There's a famous artifact (an object from the past) hidden in this inn. It's been here from the beginning of this town."

Hilga continued, "The men told me they would seek government approval to destroy this building. They claim I have no proof that this site is historical or important to anyone but me. The truth is, they are right. I do not have the artifact, and I do not know where it is hidden."

"What is it?" inquired Amina.

"It is an 18th-century goblet made of Roman glass—the only known object of its kind," explained Hilga. "The men said I must give evidence of owner-ship by finding the glass goblet. It shows the Ancient Anchor—the name of this very inn: *Die Alten Anker* in German. Five generations of innkeepers before me passed it down to the next. The previous owner hid it without telling me where he put it. Now I must find the hidden goblet or lose my inn . . . and all that I have worked for."

"Madame Hilga, the previous owner must have given you a clue," suggested Amina.

"I have searched every room in this building, even the cellar. I found nothing, until I looked through some old books on a shelf in the upstairs hallway. I turned every page of every book. I almost gave up until I looked in the pages of an old Bible. Inside I found a short poem written on a scrap of paper." She pulled the scrap paper from a pocket in her skirt and read:

Crooks under lanterns burning,
Make use of Roman learning.
Souls, young and old,
Stay close and hold
To an ancient anchoring.

"I also found a picture of an ancient coat of arms. It was rubbed on the paper with pencil from a raised imprint."

"What did the coat of arms look like?" asked Lucas. "Can you describe it?"

"I'll do better than just describe it," replied Hilga. "I have the paper behind the counter." She retrieved it quickly. "Here is what it looks like." She laid the picture, along with the poem, on the table. The children leaned over the table and studied the image. Amina made a quick sketch of the coat of arms and copied the words of the poem in her small, pocket notepad.

"I don't know what this poem means," Hilga continued. "I am a Christian, and I pray every day. Yet, I am no closer to understanding these puzzling words."

"You're a Christian believer?" asked Miguel. "We are also believers, and we want to help you. I just don't know how."

"Uh-oh," interrupted Lucas, looking at his wristwatch. "We're late for the visit to the Roman ruins. Let's go find our parents at the meeting place in the square."

"Madame Hilga, we will be back," promised Amina, stuffing her notepad in her pocket. As she followed the boys out the door, she said to Hilga, "We will find the answers you need to keep the inn. We will help you find the glass goblet and the meaning of the Ancient Anchor."

9
Searching for Clues

"Wait for me," called Amina, running through the door.

"Hurry! Run faster!" called Lucas, without breaking stride. "We need to be at the town square in 10 minutes."

The three children sprinted down the sidewalk. They soon rounded the corner to the street entering the square. The cobblestones made it difficult to run. Lucas and Miguel took care not to twist their ankles on the rounded stones as they crossed the street. Amina slipped at first, but balanced herself.

"We made it," cried Lucas, looking at his watch. "Wait a minute. According to the clock tower, we still have 15 minutes."

Amina stumbled to a stop beside the other two. "We're early! There's time to look at the coat of arms and the poem to search for clues." She pulled out the notepad from her pocket. Lucas and Miguel gathered on either side of her.

"Let's take a look," said Miguel. He was much more interested in the image and poem than Lucas, who continued to scan the crowd for his parents.

"We need to find out what the poem means," Amina began. "I wonder if the coat of arms gives us a clue to the meaning of the words."

"Let's look at it," suggested Miguel, taking the image of the coat of arms. "There's a waving banner held by a stick curved at the top. The banner has two sides. One side has a cross. It looks like the Swiss flag. On the other half of the banner there is a bird holding a twig—that seems familiar. Hey, Lucas, what does this picture of a bird remind you of?"

"Oh, that's a dove with an olive branch," responded Lucas. "I remember that from one of our memory verses in Genesis last weekend. It's from the story of Noah. He sent a dove to find land, and it returned with an olive branch. The teacher said that doves and olive branches mean 'peace follows judgment.'"

"I'm glad you remembered that," said Amina. "It helps us understand this a little more."

"Thank you. I'm glad I can help," said Lucas. He continued to watch the crowd for his parents.

Miguel said, "I wonder if the cross means judgment. Jesus died on a cross. He took our sins. Jesus took our judgment and gave us peace instead."

"The banner is attached to a stick curved at the top. That's strange," said Amina with a puzzled look. "I've seen those before in my home country. There were some boys in the neighborhood who raised sheep and goats. They walked them into the fields every morning. The boys used sticks just like that one to prod the animals."

41

Miguel agreed, "That's what they do in my country too. That is a shepherd's stick. Jesus called himself the Good Shepherd."

"That's in the Gospel of John," added Lucas. "I can't remember exactly where in the Gospel, but my father has preached about it many times."

"There's another image in the coat of arms," said Amina. "There is a huge anchor right in the middle."

"I'm glad they had an anchor ready when our boat went out of control this morning," said Lucas.

"Me too," said Miguel. "But I wonder why there is an anchor in this picture?"

"Well, this town is on a river, and where there is a river there are boats," Amina added. "So how does the anchor fit in with the rest of the images?"

"The other images are about Jesus: a dove, a cross, and a shepherd's staff," said Lucas. "But the anchor . . . it doesn't make much sense to me. I have no idea how the anchor fits in with the other stuff."

"Same with me," said Amina. "I also wonder what the image has to do with the poem."

"Read the poem again," suggested Miguel.

Amina unfolded the paper and began to recite:

> Crooks under lanterns burning,
> Make use of Roman learning.

"What is that supposed to mean?" asked Amina.

"Do you think those two strange-looking men at the inn are 'crooks'?" Lucas wondered aloud.

"I thought crooks, or thieves, hid from the light. They would not be under 'lanterns burning,'" offered Amina.

"Who, or what, are the 'crooks'?" said Miguel. "That is the question."

"Let's go to the next line," suggested Amina.

Make use of Roman learning.

"What is 'Roman learning'?" asked Amina. "Roman schools, Roman books, Roman—it's the ruins, the Roman ruins!"

"The Roman ruins," repeated Lucas. "Exactly. We will find the answer at the Roman ruins."

"There they are," said Miguel, standing up. "Our parents are coming from the other side of the square."

"They can't see us over here," said Lucas. "Let's move closer."

As the three stood up and walked across the square waving at their parents, the two strange-looking men peered from behind a wall. They followed the two families and Amina as they clattered across the cobblestones.

10
Roaming the Ruins

"It's right around the corner," said Mr. Caster, pointing to his left. "There it is."

Lucas, Miguel, and Amina dropped their jaws in amazement. In front of them was an ancient site of Roman ruins—right in the center of a modern European city.

"How old are these columns?" asked Miguel.

"This Roman outpost was built about A.D. 40," responded Miguel's father. "Many of these ruins could be between 1,500 and 2,000 years old."

"That's almost 200 of my lifetimes ago," calculated Amina.

"Let's go explore," said Lucas.

"After we look at the map and decide where to meet," said Mr. Caster. The group took a quick look at the layout of the ruins and decided to meet at the entrance in 30 minutes.

"This is amazing," said Amina, walking through the middle of ancient sculptures and columns.

"I know," said Miguel. "This plaque that tells about the history of this ancient town says it was probably founded by a friend of Julius Caesar, emperor of the Roman Empire. And just think, there's still a town on this site after all those hundreds of years."

"Look at these statues," said Lucas. "The plaque says they represented the Roman gods in their temples. That piece of flat ground over there was the original temple's foundation. Let's go check it out."

"Watch out!" hollered Miguel. "The steps are covered with loose stones. The floor of this temple was larger than my church back home in Guatemala. I wonder how high the walls were built. They could have been as big as my school's gym."

"I don't know about that," said Lucas. "But I know you're It." Lucas took off running in the opposite direction. Miguel chased him down, trying to tag him back, almost rolling off the hillside.

"I want to play too," shouted Amina. "Bet you can't catch me."

"Oh, yes I can," Lucas promised, as the three played tag on top of the temple ruins.

"OK, now I'm officially tired," said Miguel, catching his breath.

"How can you be tired," teased Lucas, resting himself on the steps of the ancient monument.

"I'm not. Let's go walk through the statue garden again," suggested Amina.

"Right now?" groaned Lucas, getting up with difficulty.

"Uh oh," warned Miguel in a hushed voice. "It's them—the two strange-looking men from the inn."

"Where?" whispered Amina, looking around nervously.

Miguel responded, "They're over by the entrance to the theater steps, but don't look directly at them. I think I saw them watching us on the temple hill."

"Let's pretend not to notice them," said Lucas. "Follow me over to the statue garden. Maybe we can lose them there."

The three navigated their way through an array of Roman statues. While tourists were busy taking photographs, and two strange men were following at a distance, they tried to slip out of sight. They stopped in front of a display that held what looked like an engraved stone tablet.

"I think we lost them," said Lucas. "I can't see them now."

"What's this?" asked Miguel. "It looks like one of the stone tablets Moses received from God with the Ten Commandments."

"I can barely read the words marked on the stone," said Amina. "I wonder what it says."

Lucas said, "Here's a plaque that tells what it says."

"The plaque says the words are written in Latin," said Amina. "It reads, 'To the beloved Eusstata [oos-STAH-tah], my beloved wife of 65 years, from Amatus [ah-MAH-toos].'"

Then Lucas continued to read from the plaque. "'This grave marker is from a husband to his wife. The symbol of the anchor at the top of the tombstone was a common sign on Christian graves. It is the earliest evidence for the presence of Christianity in western Europe.'"

"That is amazing," remarked Miguel, speaking for all of them. "'The earliest known evidence for Christi-

anity,' it says. It dates this tombstone around A.D. 350. That's more than 16 centuries ago."

"Just think," began Lucas, "there used to be a huge temple over there. It was built in honor of these statues of their Roman gods. And here, among all those false gods, a Christian believer lived and died. What an amazing story about God! He is everywhere."

"Hold on a second," whispered Amina. "You're talking about the symbol of an anchor."

"What did you say?" asked Miguel. He was still thinking about those ancient believers.

"There's an ancient anchor on this tombstone. It says, *'Die Alten Anker,'* just like the name of Hilga's inn," said Amina, pulling the notepad out of her pocket. She read, *"'Make use of Roman learning.'"*

Lucas responded, "'Roman learning' was in Latin, like the words written on this tombstone."

Amina read the next line, *"'Souls, young and old.'"*

Miguel explained, "That means people like us, young Christians, and old souls like Eusstata."

Amina read the last two lines, *"'Stay close and hold To an ancient anchoring.'"*

Miguel continued, "Believers need to stay faithful to God, even when it is hard. The 'ancient anchoring' means Christianity. Christ is the anchor—the Ancient Anchor."

"We have to get back to the inn," said Lucas.

"You're right," said Amina. "We have to tell Hilga that we found the meaning of the poem. We found the clue to find the hidden goblet. Hilga wasn't looking in the right place."

"No, I mean we have to get back to the inn, right now," said Lucas, urgently. "Those strange-looking men are standing on the other side of those statues. And they keep looking this way."

"Let's walk over to our parents and tell them to meet us at *Die Alten Anker,*" suggested Miguel. "Then we can sneak away before the men know we are leaving."

They walked as patiently and innocently as they could toward their parents, but their hearts were beating faster than their footsteps.

11

The Final Clue

"Whew! Here's the inn, and I don't think they saw us," said Amina, glancing over her shoulder toward the town square.

"Quick! Let's get off the street right away," urged Lucas.

The three friends ducked through the blue door of the inn.

"Hilga!" yelled Lucas, as he entered the café. "Hilga, are you here?"

Miguel went to look into the side room, while Amina peeked through the kitchen door. Lucas walked toward the stairs, continuing to call out for Hilga.

"Hil . . ." began Lucas.

"Who's calling my name?" interrupted a voice from the top of the open staircase.

"It's Lucas, along with Miguel and Amina," he explained, as Hilga came down the stairs.

"Oh, I'm glad to see you," said Hilga. "Have you figured out the coat of arms and the poem? Can you help me find the hidden goblet?"

"Yes, we can," Lucas assured her. "Amina discovered the meaning of the poem."

Lucas called out for Amina and Miguel. All four sat down in chairs around a small table as Amina explained the meaning of the poem.

"But that still doesn't give us the location of the goblet," shrugged Hilga, disappointed.

"There is one more clue," Amina reminded them. "It's the very first line. *'Crooks under lanterns burning.'*"

"I thought those two strange men were the crooks. They are trying to steal this inn away from Hilga," said Lucas.

"That's only one meaning for the word 'crook,'" said Amina. "A crook can mean a shepherd's stick or staff."

"There's a shepherd's staff holding the banner on the side of the coat of arms," added Lucas.

"What does a shepherd's staff have to do with the hidden goblet?" Miguel inquired.

"'Crooks under lanterns burning,'" repeated Hilga thoughtfully. "What flag is waving in the breeze outside the inn? It's the flag of Basel. On it is an image of a shepherd's staff. The flag is flying right underneath a street lamp."

"A lamp made out of glass," added Miguel.

"Are you thinking what I'm thinking?" asked Lucas.

"I think so," said Amina confidently. "Hilga, do you have a ladder?"

"A ladder? Yes, I have one in the cellar," replied Hilga. "Boys, will you help me get it?"

A few minutes later, they were all standing in front of *Die Alten Anker*. Amina instructed, "Lucas, put the ladder right next to the lamp. Hold it steady while Miguel climbs up and unscrews the lamp from the metal post. Please be careful."

Miguel slowly made his way up the ladder, rung by rung.

"Whoa! Watch it!" cried Lucas. "You almost tipped over the ladder!"

"I know, I know," said Miguel, barely keeping his balance. "Just keep the ladder straight. I'm almost to the place where I can reach the lamp."

"I've almost got it loosened," Miguel said mostly to himself.

"Careful now, don't drop . . . look out!" Lucas shouted.

Amina dropped the notepad and jumped under the glass lamp as it landed in her hands. She cradled it in her arms as if it were a little puppy.

"Here it is," she said to Hilga.

"Look at the engraving on the side of the lamp," said Hilga. "It looks just like the pencil drawing I showed you earlier today."

Amina said, "It's the hidden goblet. The glass lamp was the hidden goblet—only it was hidden in plain sight."

"Uh oh!" exclaimed Miguel from 10 feet up. "It looks like we have visitors coming."

Lucas helped Miguel down the ladder while the strange-looking men walked up to *Die Alten Anker.*

"What is that you have there?" asked one of the men.

"It is just what I needed to make you leave me and my inn alone," replied Hilga. "Now, if you will excuse us, please. I need to go make some free hot chocolate for my new friends here."

After Miguel and Lucas lugged the ladder back into the cellar, they sat down with Hilga and Amina to enjoy a smooth and steamy cup of hot Swiss chocolate. They could not stop looking at the centuries-old-goblet. They knew it had saved Hilga's café and inn from being destroyed.

It wasn't long before a few cold and thirsty customers entered the café. One of them spoke.

"Hello, kids," greeted Mr. Caster. "Did we miss anything?"

12
Almost Home

"Can't we play just one more game of Uno before we get to the train station?" pleaded Amina. "I really like this game."

"Uno! I'm down to one card," said Miguel, just before he saw a chance to lay it down. "I finally won!"

"That was fun," said Amina. "I'm glad you taught me how to play Uno. Actually, I'm glad for what both of you taught me on this trip. I learned a lot about God, and how to be a Christian. I'm very grateful."

"It was something we were glad to do," said Lucas. "I wouldn't have missed how you discovered Jesus for anything else in the world."

"Me either," chimed in Miguel. "We are glad to be your friends, as well as a friend in Christ. It was quite a trip—by train, boat, and on foot. Can you believe we helped our new friend Hilga keep *Die Alten Anker* from being torn down?"

"It made me feel good to help her," agreed Lucas.

"It was amazing how the ancient anchor on the Roman tombstone unlocked the rest of the clues," said

Amina. "I still can't believe we saw the first sign of Christianity in Europe on this trip."

Flipping his winning card in the air, Miguel said, "And here's to *uno mas* [MAHS]—that's Spanish for 'one more'—one more Christian in Europe."

Lucas and Miguel squeezed Amina in one-arm hugs before she left the train at the Geneva station.

"Well, Amina, how was the trip?" asked her father, as they settled into his car.

"How long is the drive home?" answered Amina with another question.

"Oh, probably 90 minutes," he replied.

"I don't think that is enough time," smiled Amina. "It will take *forever* to tell you all that took place on this trip."